asking nothing, giving everything

Prayer book for everyone

BHAKTI BUDDY

INDIA • SINGAPORE • MALAYSIA

Copyright © Bhakti Buddy 2024
All Rights Reserved.

ISBN   979-8-89277-844-2

This book has been published with all efforts taken to make the material error-free after the consent of the author. However, the author and the publisher do not assume and hereby disclaim any liability to any party for any loss, damage, or disruption caused by errors or omissions, whether such errors or omissions result from negligence, accident, or any other cause.

While every effort has been made to avoid any mistake or omission, this publication is being sold on the condition and understanding that neither the author nor the publishers or printers would be liable in any manner to any person by reason of any mistake or omission in this publication or for any action taken or omitted to be taken or advice rendered or accepted on the basis of this work. For any defect in printing or binding the publishers will be liable only to replace the defective copy by another copy of this work then available.

Acknowledgment

Every word and thought in this book is made possible by the boundless grace of the divine. The guidance has been a constant light in my journey, and I humbly acknowledge that everything I do reflects this divine grace.

Contents

Prayers Beyond Desires

Imagine you receive an invitation, and upon reading it, you immediately start creating a list of things you want from the event.

You think about the delicious food you expect, the opportunity to network with certain people, and even the chance to showcase your achievements.

Your focus is on what you can gain from attending, and your engagement is transactional—you're essentially entering into a social contract with your friend, expecting specific benefits in return for your presence.

This scenario resembles the concept of transactional prayer in the spiritual context. In transactional prayers, individuals approach the divine with a similar mindset, sharing a list of desires and requests.

It's a planned interaction where the worshipper expects specific good things from the divine, similar to the expectations one has when attending an event. The act of praying becomes a sort of negotiation, where the seeker seeks fulfillment of their needs in exchange for their devotion.

Now, consider a different approach. Imagine getting the same invitation, but instead of focusing on what you can get, you feel a strong sense of thankfulness and affection for your friend.

You attend the party not with a list of expectations but with a heart full of appreciation for the friendship you share.

Your presence is a celebration of the bond you have, and you welcome the evening with openness and joy. There's no hidden agenda or checklist of desires; it's a genuine, selfless expression of love and connection.

This scenario connects with the concept of prayers beyond desires. In these kinds of prayers, individuals approach the divine with deep thankfulness and love, similar to going to a party with a heart full of gratefulness for a friend.

The prayer becomes a celebration of the spiritual bond shared with the divine, and the seekers' expectation is not dependent on a checklist of desires.

It's a sincere, unselfish expression of love and connection, highlighting the transformative power of prayers that go beyond the transactional world.

This book is about discovering prayers that go beyond requesting things. The prayers are like a beautiful song of thanks, love, and giving everything to the divine.

The focus is on celebrating the special connection without thinking about what we can get in return. Each prayer in the book is like a joyful dance with the divine that doesn't involve trying to negotiate or secretly wanting something.

It's an invitation to experience the type of prayers that goes beyond just wanting stuff—a pure, open-hearted connection and a happy celebration of the special bond we share with the divine.

The intent of the book is not to diminish the importance of transactional prayers—they are as precious as any other kind of prayer. Whether you're expressing gratitude, seeking guidance, or making specific requests, each prayer has its place and is special.

Imagine you're in a big kitchen preparing a meal. In this kitchen, every dish you cook represents a different type of prayer. Now, think of transactional prayers as one kind of dish and prayers beyond desires as another.

Transactional prayers are like dishes you cook because you're hungry for something specific. It's like saying, "I'll prepare this meal if I get exactly what I'm craving." These prayers are important, just like certain dishes are necessary for a meal to be satisfying.

Now, prayers beyond desires are like a different set of dishes that you prepare not because you're craving something particular, but simply because you love the act of cooking.

You make these dishes not expecting a specific taste in return but because you enjoy the entire process. These prayers focus on relishing the joy of the kitchen without aiming for a particular flavor.

Both types of dishes are delightful and have their place in the kitchen. So the intention of the book is not to overlook the importance of preparing specific meals (transactional prayers), but to highlight how wonderful it is to enjoy the entire cooking experience (prayers beyond desires).

There's something truly special and transformative about enjoying the process without always craving a specific taste. It's like finding the magic in the kitchen itself, not just in the dishes you hope to taste.

Prayer Book for Everyone

Regardless of the form or name you worship, what truly matters is the intensity of your emotion and love for the divine. In devotion, every name carries power, and every heart filled with love holds the potential for a profound sacred connection. What's most important is your strong devotion, loyalty, and sincerity in remembering the divine name.

The heart of devotion lies in genuinely remembering the holy name. It's a reminder to be completely focused during worship, letting the name resonate inside, and filling each syllable with love and meaning. In this deep act of remembrance, a worshipper forms a direct link with the divine, where the lord's name transforms into a sacred vibration within the soul.

The real power of devotion is its ability to break down barriers and embrace the unity of all spiritual paths. It encourages individuals to see the divine spark in every form and appreciate how our differences make our shared spiritual adventure more interesting.

In the world of devotion, what matters the most is the depth of emotion, the purity of love, and the loyal commitment to one's spiritual path. These things build a strong foundation between the worshipper and the divine.

Imagine someone deeply involved in prayer, going beyond how they look on the outside because of their religious beliefs. In that special moment, the person praying becomes a channel for love, sharing feelings as gifts to the divine.

It recognizes that love is the universal language of the heart, acting as a connection between the person praying and the divine, regardless of how someone expresses their faith in terms of language or culture.

For a devotee, love is the most important thing. This book is like a warm hug for all devotees who hold their divine close to their hearts. It doesn't matter which divine you like or whose name you trust; what matters is the love and devotion you have inside you.

Every prayer, every time you show your love to your chosen divine, and every moment you think about them, they are all very special, no matter whose name you say. Think of it like different colors coming together to make a beautiful painting—your devotion is like those colors, unique and beautiful.

Your devotion, your love, is the heart of your inward journey. It's like a friendly light that helps you get closer to your chosen divine. Imagine different kinds of musical notes coming together to create a lovely tune; that's how our different forms of devotion come together to make a wonderful feeling of love for the divine.

So, when you read these prayers, remember that your love and devotion are very important. Every time you pray with love, offer your heart with love or just think about your chosen divine with love, it brings you closer to them.

In this book's prayers, let's celebrate and be happy about how much we care about the divine and love our beliefs. While reading the prayers, think of your heart as a beautiful garden where your love for the divine grows like colorful flowers.

Each petal is a special way you show your strong love for what you believe in. These flowers, like a special story of love and dedication, tell a tale that goes beyond the limits of words and culture. They create a safe place where the universal language of love is the most important.

As you take care of this garden, see each flower as a symbol of a different part of your dedication. One flower might be like the roots of your strong belief, keeping you connected to the divine. Its stem, strong and steady, shows the committed choice that holds your spiritual journey, no matter the way you follow.

Another flower could show the warm feelings in your heart when you pray or think deeply. The soft petals of these feelings move with a gentle breeze, making a happy dance that shows the little details of your love for the divine. These feelings are like threads that carefully make the story of your dedication, a language that feels right beyond any specific religion or culture.

In this colorful garden, different flowers show the many spiritual paths and ways people love the divine. Each special tradition, belief, or personal idea of the divine is shown by a flower, all living together peacefully. The beauty of this garden isn't about being the same but about enjoying being different, showing that the universal heart of dedication is part of everyone's shared human connection.

As these flowers grow, their sweet smells mix, making a wonderful scent that represents the shared energy of dedication in your spiritual space. Whether you follow a certain form or have a mix of spiritual ideas, the nice smell of your love goes beyond your garden, reaching out to connect with the bigger garden of humanity.

Imagine the roots of these flowers twisting together under the ground, making a complicated network of connections. This network shows the common heart of dedication that brings all seekers together, going beyond the outer differences. It shows the shared thing—a universal human wish to connect with the divine.

Taking care of this garden is a spiritual practice on its own. Your care and attention, like a careful gardener, help the flowers grow. Looking after your garden means being present, thinking about yourself, and choosing to make a happy place where the divine can be seen in many ways.

Think of the prayers in this book like tiny seeds in your commitment garden. Each prayer is a small seed waiting to grow into a unique flower, adding its color and smell to your spiritual space. Just like a gardener eagerly watches for signs of new growth, anticipate the growth of wisdom, peace, and understanding from these heartfelt words.

Think of each prayer as a little tale shared by the flowers in your garden. Some prayers might be like bright red flowers, showing passion and excitement for your spiritual journey. Others could be soft blues, bringing a sense of calm and peace. The diversity in these prayers shows the different ways people express their devotion, creating an artwork of feelings and experiences.

As you read the prayers, picture the petals of each flower opening up, revealing the beauty inside. Similarly, let the words of the prayers uncover the layers of meaning and connection in your heart. Each prayer is like a stroke on the canvas of your spiritual garden, adding to the masterpiece of your personal and shared devotion.

In the garden of prayers, let your mind roam and explore the different scents and colors that emerge. Some prayers may resonate deeply with your feelings, while others introduce new perspectives and insights. Accept this mix of thoughts and feelings just like you'd welcome a bunch of flowers in your garden, understanding that beauty comes from the interaction of different ways people express love and devotion.

Just as a gardener cares for every plant, water these prayers with your attention and reflection. Let the messages sink into the rich soil of your heart, helping you understand your spiritual journey better. Like a well-maintained garden, let the prayers inspire growth, strength, and a continuous flowering of your connection with the divine.

Bhakti Buddy: Why This Pen Name

In the big world of different beliefs, where everyone has their unique perspectives, I found a purpose—to be a friend of every devotee. I didn't just want to watch; I wanted to be a friend to every devoted person going through the ups and downs of love and devotion. And that's how the purpose got a name: Bhakti Buddy.

Bhakti is more than just a word; it's a deep expression of love and devotion aimed at making the divine happy. It's like turning our feelings into actions, much like when we do things to bring joy to someone we love. Think about saying, "I love you, and I'll do things that make you happy." In Bhakti, it's this sincere commitment to show love through our actions, connecting with the divine. It's like saying: "I really care about you, and everything I do is to bring joy to your heart."

And a buddy isn't just a regular friend; it's a reliable companion who's there for you no matter what. A buddy is someone you can trust, someone who understands you without needing to say much.

It's like having a friend by your side to share all sorts of moments and provide strong support when you need it. Essentially, a buddy is that dependable friend who makes life's journey a bit easier, and a bit more fun.

Now, when we blend Bhakti and Buddy, it creates a beautiful picture. Bhakti Buddy is a mix of love and friendship on a spiritual journey. It represents a promise to express deep love and devotion, much like the strong connection we have with our divine source. Imagine a friend who not only understands your feelings but also walks with you on your spiritual path. Bhakti Buddy is that trustworthy companion, a servant who joins you in celebrating your beliefs and supports you through tough times.

It's more than just a label; it's a living example of the idea that showing love for the divine is like having a good friend by your side. When life gets tough, Bhakti Buddy symbolizes strong support, just like a true friend who gets you and embraces your story. It's an invitation to a heartfelt friendship where love and companionship come together on the special journey of devotion.

So, when I say 'I'm Bhakti Buddy,' I mean I want to be a friend to everyone who shares this beautiful bond of devotion, no matter what you believe in. I want to connect with that deep love and strong dedication in every devotee. I understand that in every faith, there's a shared thread—a constant devotion and a deep connection to what we cherish. It's like a warm, meaningful friendship with the divine and each other.

Imagine a big school where students with different thoughts come together. I'm just one student there, eager to learn from everyone, no matter what their beliefs are. I'm not a teacher giving lessons. I'm just like you, a learner ready to understand and grow from what others believe. When I say Bhakti Buddy, I mean I'm here to be a friend on this journey, learning and growing with you. I'm here to listen, understand, and be a support.

So, in every prayer, every word, and every moment, Bhakti Buddy aims to be the friend who walks beside you, capturing the love that connects us, the surrender that sets us free, and the gratitude that fills our hearts. It's a beautiful blend of expressing love and finding comfort in a reliable friend, creating a pleasant tune in the melody of life's spiritual journey.

Anyone can be a Bhakti Buddy

Any person walking the path of devotion is, essentially, a Bhakti Buddy. Whether it's you, me, or anyone who carries that love and dedication within, we're all Bhakti Buddies. This journey isn't exclusive; it's an open invitation for everyone to walk together, learn, understand, and flourish in this beautiful harmony of faith and love.

Devotion is not a club with limited membership—it's a universal language of the heart. Every individual, regardless of their beliefs, carries the capacity for love, which is the very essence of Bhakti. It's a shared trait that unites us on a deep level, going beyond the boundaries of differing perspectives.

In a world where differences can sometimes create distance, Bhakti stands as a unifying force. It serves as a gentle reminder that, deep down, we all share common desires—for love, peace, and understanding. Bhakti Buddy isn't just a name; it represents a commitment to being a good friend, understanding, and providing support. It extends an open invitation to let the inborn kindness within each of us shine.

So, let's acknowledge and celebrate the Bhakti Buddy within us. Let's enjoy the shared journey, walking together, and celebrating the love and beliefs we have in common. This isn't just my book; it's OUR book—a collective narrative of shared love and devotion. Together, let's explore this beautiful path, building a sense of togetherness and unity, and creating a story that reflects the universal aspects of faith and love that connect us all.

Power of Prayers in Today's Age

In today's fast-paced and technology-driven world, with constant information flow, work pressures, and the always-present digital buzz, many of us can understand the feeling of being isolated and disconnected from others.

We're all searching for something more—a sense of meaning, a genuine connection, and a break from the never-ending demands of our modern lives. It's precisely in these moments of digital chaos that the power of prayer shines through.

Pause for a moment and picture the hectic race we're all part of today.

We're constantly chasing deadlines, scrolling through social media, and battling the rising tide of anxiety. You might wonder, does prayer even have a place in this high-tech, fast-paced world?

The truth is, it's not only relevant but profoundly essential.

In today's world, prayers are like the charging station for the spirit, a place where the battery of our souls reconnects to a divine source. In a world flooded with notifications and alarms, prayer is the super special zone where we plug in, allowing our inner light to recharge, brightening the path ahead. It's the sacred USB port that links us to something greater, way beyond our screens and pixels.

In this sacred space of prayer, our souls become like smartphones in need of recharging. The constant demands of modern life drain us, much like apps consume the battery of our devices.

Prayer, then, is the moment we connect to the cosmic power source, going beyond the limitations of regular life. It's like a wireless charging pad for the spirit, making us feel energized and ready to rock in today's world.

Just as a USB port makes it super easy for data to move smoothly between devices, prayer serves as a special link through which our innermost thoughts, fears, and aspirations are shared with the divine.

It's a data transfer of the soul, going beyond the bandwidth of regular communication. In this holy exchange, we download a sense of purpose, upload our burdens, and sync our existence with higher energy, creating a spiritual connection stronger than any Wi-Fi signal.

Consider prayer as the antivirus software for the soul, protecting us from the viruses of despair, doubt, and disconnection that slide into our mental and emotional operating systems. When we pray, it's like starting a spiritual scan, identifying and eliminating the malware that threatens our inner well-being. It's a firewall against the negativity that bombards us daily, ensuring the integrity of our spiritual core.

The sacred USB port of prayer is also a universal adapter, going beyond all the languages and traditions. No matter what language you speak or how you do things, praying is like a super universal language that brings together all kinds of spiritual vibes.

It's like a language your heart understands, letting people from different walks of life connect with the big spiritual network and feel something amazing together.

The divine USB connection becomes a source code for personal transformation. It's like a super important update for your inner self, adding bits of wisdom, kindness, and strength.

Every time you connect through prayer, you get the latest version of your spiritual software, turning into someone who can handle all the tricky stuff of life with style and understanding.

Think of prayer not just as a regular charging spot, but as a way for our regular self to connect with the powerful mainframe in the universe. It's like updating our spiritual software to keep our souls strong, similar to maintaining gadgets for the challenges of the modern world.

In our busy lives, prayer is like a reset for the soul. It reminds us that, despite all the hurrying, there's a peaceful spot inside us for comfort and meaning. In a world valuing speed over deep thought, prayer allows us to pause, think, and connect with something beyond what we can see and measure easily.

Think of prayer as a GPS for the soul, guiding us through life's complicated journey. Just like a GPS gives directions, prayer is like a map for our spirit, helping us face problems, make good choices, and discover our purpose. It's like a compass pointing us towards doing the right thing, leading us on a journey to learn more about ourselves and feel fulfilled.

Prayer is powerful not just for one person but for everyone together. It's similar to how a bunch of devices work better when connected. When we all pray together, it's like we create a shared energy that goes beyond just one person.

Imagine prayer as a software update for people and society. When we pray, it's like we're downloading feelings of understanding, acceptance, and taking care of each other. It's like everyone getting a group update that goes beyond where they are from or what they believe, making a global awareness that shows how we're all connected.

And prayer isn't just for personal or group change—it can affect the whole world. It's like dropping a pebble in the water and watching the ripples go out. The good energy from prayer adds up, creating more kindness and goodwill. In a world struggling with challenges ranging from environmental crises to social injustices, the collective power of prayer becomes a force for positive change.

Prayer serves as a bridge between the finite nature of our existence and the infinite possibilities that lie beyond. It's something timeless that doesn't depend on what year it is or what gadgets we have. In a world that likes to focus on what's outside, prayer is a way to look inside, reminding us that, even when everything goes crazy, we can find a quiet place of peace, purpose, and a connection with something bigger than us.

How to Approach This Book

The prayers in this book are not about wanting or asking for anything. Instead, the main idea is to love and appreciate the divine's presence. It's like having a heart-to-heart chat without asking for anything specific. It's not about saying, "Give me this" or "Help me with that." It's more like enjoying the moment and feeling a strong connection without expecting anything in return.

Think of these prayers as moments of thinking, appreciation, and recognition of the divine in various forms. It's about appreciating the beauty of life, acknowledging the impact of the divine in our lives, and expressing thanks for the simple yet significant moments in our human experience. Essentially, it's a kind of spiritual connection that aims to strengthen the relationship with the divine without attaching conditions or expectations.

This approach to prayer shifts the focus from a transactional mindset to one of mindfulness and being present. It will encourage you to be fully engaged in the moment, recognizing the divine not just in times of need but also in moments of happiness, quietness, and everyday occurrences. It's a way of building an ongoing connection and conversation, making prayer a complete and fulfilling practice that goes beyond specific requests.

As you start this journey, remember it's your unique experience. Read the book in a way that feels right for you—there are no strict rules. Enjoy the special moments in each prayer, and relish the richness of your exploration.

While you are free to explore the experience, here are some points to keep in mind as you read these prayers, enhancing the depth of your spiritual journey.

Feel the Emotions

Think of each prayer in this special book as a little package filled with emotions that can touch your heart. It's a bit like when you hear a song, and it makes you feel happy, inspired, or just calm. These prayers are like that—they're like musical notes of feelings.

Just like how a song can make people feel all sorts of things, these prayers can do the same for you. Some prayers are like the happiest part of a song, filling your heart with so much love that it might make you cry a little. It's a good kind of crying, though—like when you see something incredibly sweet or touching.

Then some prayers are like a happy dance for your heart. They make you think about all the awesome things in your life and make you feel thankful. It's like counting your blessings and realizing how much good stuff you have around you.

And when life gets a bit tough, some prayers act like a comforting hug. They make you feel calm and peaceful, like a warm blanket for your heart. It's like having a friend who understands and is there to make you feel better.

So, when you open this book and read these prayers, it's like pressing play on a playlist of emotions. Each prayer has its special tune—a melody of love, gratitude, and peace that can make your heart dance, reflect, and find comfort in different ways. It's like your own little concert of feelings, waiting to be discovered.

Remember that there's no one right way to understand or feel them. It's okay to feel any emotion as you read. These prayers aren't tied to any rules or beliefs; they're an invitation to explore your feelings and discover what touches your heart the most.

Discover Your Unique Connection

Your connection with the divine is as unique as you are. Whether you see it as a guiding light, a comforting friend, or in any other way, these prayers make room for your expression.

So, enjoy the liberty to uncover and nurture your special connection, without any limits. Let these prayers be like a friendly hug, supporting you on your extraordinary journey to understanding and connecting with the divine in your amazing way.

Imagine these prayers like a handy toolbox, giving you the freedom to create your unique spiritual connection in a way that feels right to your heart. You're not stuck in a set pattern. Instead, these prayers act like buddies on your journey, appreciating the beauty in how people see and feel the divine in their way.

Go ahead and discover your magic within these prayers. Imagine them as keys that unlock the door to your unique relationship with the divine. It's like finding your secret code, spoken in the language of your heart. These prayers are here to celebrate the diversity of connections, reminding you that your way is the perfect way for you.

Explore at Your Speed

Think of this book as that timeless friend who doesn't care about being on time or following strict rules. It's like having a buddy who's always there, ready to hang out whenever you want to take a moment to think, find inspiration, or simply have a peaceful break in your day.

This friend, the book, understands your schedule, seamlessly fits into your routine, and it's always prepared to share its bits of wisdom and comforting words whenever you decide to open it up and see what's inside.

It's like having a friend that doesn't pressure you with deadlines or demands. Instead, it respects your time and is available whenever you need it.

Whether you want to read a page or two in the morning, during lunch, or right before bed, this friend is happy to be there, offering insights and a sense of calm whenever you decide to spend time with it. It's a companion that understands and adapts, making sure it fits into your life in a way that feels just right for you.

Don't Just Read; Pause and Think

Once you've read a prayer, take a little break for yourself. Step away from everything for a bit and let those words stay with you, bouncing around inside you like echoes in a quiet cave.

Find a nice, comfortable spot where there aren't too many things going on, maybe your special spot, and just sit there. Imagine the prayer resonating through you, kind of like when you drop a stone in a calm pond, and the ripples spread out.

It's like creating a peaceful, quiet space where the words can settle in and become a part of how you feel and think. Just take a moment to let those echoes of the prayer sink into you, almost like a warm, gentle hug for your thoughts and feelings.

This special time lets the words become more than just words; they become like a quiet friend, staying with you and making a comfy home within you.

Thinking is like taking a little trip inside yourself. It's not just about thinking about the words; it's like going on an adventure in your thoughts. Ask yourself how each prayer fits into your life at this moment. Does it make you feel better when things are hard or make the good times even happier? Find out the different meanings, and look into the details that might not be super clear at first.

As you connect the prayer to your experiences, problems, and happy moments, it becomes more than just words on a page. It turns into a guide for your everyday life, kind of like a friendly map showing you the way in your story.

Spread the Magic (Most Important)

Have honest and deep conversations with your close ones about how these prayers make a difference in your lives. Tell them what you feel, and listen to what they feel too. This shared experience is like creating a friendly wave of positivity that doesn't just help each person grow spiritually but also helps the whole group grow.

When you talk openly with the people you care about, it's like planting seeds of good vibes. You share your thoughts and hear theirs, and it's like these positive thoughts start to spread among everyone. It's not just about you becoming a better person; it's about everyone becoming better together.

Exploring together, it's not just about learning more; it's also about creating a sense of being together and supporting each other. When people in the group share their different ways of looking at things, it's like discovering new meanings that maybe you didn't notice on your own. Everyone in the group becomes part of a team, working together to build a big picture of understanding.

Think of it like putting together a puzzle with your friends. Each person has a puzzle piece, and when you bring them all together, you see the whole picture. Exploring together is a bit like that—everyone in the group brings their ideas and thoughts. And when you put them together, it forms a complete picture that's much richer and more interesting than if you were figuring things out on your own.

So, when you explore with others, you're not just learning; you're creating a shared space where everyone's ideas count and contribute to a bigger and better understanding of things. It's like teamwork in understanding and appreciating the special magic in these prayers.

Prayer Themes

In this book, we're going on a journey to understand our special connection with the divine. Imagine a story with deep feelings, where every word is like a sweet song in your heart. As we read, let's feel the love and devotion guiding us through prayers and the dance of our emotions.

Think about standing at the beginning of a special place where the air feels exciting, and even the silence has a voice. In these pages, we'll learn about three important themes in our prayers: Love, Surrender, and Gratitude. These aren't just big ideas; they're like the heartbeats of our journey, making our thoughts meaningful and connecting us to the divine.

But before we dive into these themes, let's take a moment at the start of our journey. Remember the times when your heart felt warm, or you wished for something more than what you could touch? That's where our journey begins.

Remember the times when the heaviness of the world seemed to go away, if only for a little while, as you looked at the sky or whispered comforting words. These are the divine moments, gently telling us to explore our feelings. In this journey, we find comfort, a purpose, and a story of emotions waiting to be uncovered.

Now, as we start this adventure, let your true feelings mix with the strength of your faith. The themes we're talking about aren't like faraway stars; they're like stars inside us, guiding us through our spiritual journey. So, with an open heart and a curious mind, let's embrace the love, surrender, and gratitude, letting them shape our prayers and the music of our connection with the divine.

Love: Embracing the Divine Connection

Love is more than a feeling; it's a deep force that forms the very heart of our connection with the divine. It's the warmth that wraps around us like a cozy hug, going beyond just how we feel.

As we look into love, we'll uncover its amazing power, figuring out how it connects our human side with the divine. This invites us to talk intimately with the divine, a moment where we show vulnerability by saying, "I love you, and I feel your love around me."

Love becomes a language beyond words, something our souls understand, binding us into the delicate pattern of the universe. Just like the bright sunrise after a long night, love can change us and light up our spiritual path.

Surrender: Jumping Into the Adventure of Faith

Surrender is like stepping into the unknown with unwavering trust. It's the act of saying, "I release my grip, for I trust in your divine plan." It is not about giving up; it's about finding calmness in the act of letting go.

It's like standing at the edge of a vast ocean, feeling the waves carry you gently. Surrender evokes deep emotions because it frees us from the chains of fear and doubt.

Imagine holding onto a heavy backpack full of worries and fears. Surrender is like taking off that backpack and feeling a sense of relief. It's about trusting that things will work out, even when life gets tough. When you surrender, you release control and allow life to guide you during a storm.

Gratitude: Creating Colorful Expressions of Thanks

Gratitude is a heartfelt way of saying "Thank you" to the divine for all the wonderful blessings we've received. It's like a group of happy voices singing together in joy.

When we express gratitude in our prayers, it's as if we're using a brush to paint a picture of appreciation. It's a way of saying, "I'm truly thankful for the beauty, love, and simple joys in life." It's our heart's way of feeling content and happy.

Gratitude fills us with positive feelings because it helps us see all the amazing things in life. It's like a harmonious orchestra of good emotions that make us feel uplifted. When we express gratitude, it's like admiring a stunning sunset that paints the sky with breathtaking colors, leaving us wondering about the beauty in the world.

Beautiful Dance of Themes

Think of these themes as partners in a lovely dance, moving smoothly in harmony. Picture it like a captivating, flowing dance where each step leads gracefully to the next, creating a sweet melody of feelings within our hearts.

Love starts this beautiful dance. Imagine this step as a gentle move into the arms of a higher power's love. In this dance, love becomes the foundation, a comforting hug that encourages us to release our grip on worries and fears. As we trust in the love that surrounds us, a sense of openness arises, forming the basis for a deeper connection with the divine.

Following the rhythm of love, the next move in this dance is surrender. It's like another beautiful step, a deliberate act of letting go and placing trust in the divine plan. Surrender brings with it a deep sense of calmness, like the feeling of being carried by gentle waves at the edge of a vast ocean.

In this part of the dance, we set aside the weight of troubling thoughts, finding comfort in the act of surrender. Trusting that things will unfold positively, even in the middle of life's challenges, becomes a meaningful expression of this graceful move.

Completing the dance is gratitude, the final and most enchanting part of the sequence. It's like a gentle breeze that touches the dance floor, making the entire experience even more beautiful. Expressing gratitude is like painting lively strokes of appreciation.

It helps us see the good in everything around us, transforming the dance into a celebration of life's blessings. Gratitude deepens our capacity for love, creating a harmonious rhythm that lifts the entire dance to new heights.

These themes, blended in this sweet dance, are more than just words. They form the very pulse of our existence, reminding us to pause and enjoy the magnificence of life.

In this dance, we find comfort in releasing worries, discovering peace in openness, and recognizing the extraordinary in everyday moments. It's a rhythm that underscores our journey, encouraging us to cherish each step, emotion, and word.

This journey isn't about reaching a specific place; it's an invitation to enjoy every step of the dance. It encourages us to embrace each emotion as a note in the melody of our lives. As we spin through the dance of these themes, we discover the sweet beauty within ourselves and the world around us.

So, let's step forward with open hearts, ready to explore the marvelous world of emotions together, immersed in the timeless dance of our spiritual existence.

LOVE

I don't want to fall in love with you, I want to rise in love with you. I don't want to put any conditions. I just want to give everything to you without any limitations or exceptions. You complete me. You give me the happiness and strength to move forward in life. I cannot and do not want to see anything beyond you.

When I realized that I wanted to be with you forever, it was like a light bulb turned on in my head. Suddenly, my life had a new purpose, and all that mattered was my relationship with you. I felt a strong desire to be close to you all the time. It was like a fire was burning inside me, urging me to run towards you with all my might. I knew it wouldn't be easy, but I was ready for it because my love for you was all-consuming.

If I got a flower every time I thought of you, I'd have enough flowers to create an endless garland for your feet. I'd then love to walk with you in that garden of flowers forever and give you each flower as a symbol of my love for you. I would also welcome others to join me in that beautiful place and pay their respects to your divine presence. I would also share my story of how I found you and the remarkable ways in which you've influenced my life.

Even if the sun didn't shine and the mountains went away in the sea, my love for you wouldn't change. I'll always stick by you, even if the stars fell or the oceans dried up and the earth turned to sand.

Even if everything stopped or time froze, I'd still find a way to be with you. Even if the wind refused to blow, and the rivers decided not to flow, I'd still cherish you each day, in every little, lovely way.

Even if the moon lost its glow, and the night forgot to show, I'd hold you close, never apart, with you forever in my heart. Even if the rain forgot to fall, and the flowers stopped growing tall, my love for you would still stand strong, like the melody in a happy song.

When I'm sad, I think of you. When I'm happy, I think of you. When I'm lonely, I think of you. When I'm excited, I think of you. When I'm anxious, I think of you. When I'm grateful, I think of you. When I'm confused, I think of you. When I'm inspired, I think of you. In all these different situations, one thing remains constant—I think of you because you've become an important part of my thoughts and feelings.

When I say "I love you," it's not just a feeling that comes and goes. It means I'm really devoted to you. These three words are very special to me because they show how much I care about our relationship. When I say "I love you," it's like I'm sharing my innermost feelings with you and letting you see who I really am. When I say "I love you," it's like I'm recognizing that you are the source of all love and goodness in the world and that my love for you is a reflection of your love for me.

My affection for you is a strong energy that flows through my body, urging me to do things that might seem illogical to others. But to me, it's the most natural thing in the world. When I'm with you, my heart beats faster, my mind becomes clearer, and my spirit is filled with joy. It's as if I've discovered my true calling—to love and serve you with every part of me. I'll continue to love and cherish you for as long as I live.

I love you with all my heart. I give myself to you completely without thinking about what I'll get back. My love for you is limitless, and I give to you with all my heart. I hold nothing back, and my love for you flows like a river that never stops. I surrender myself completely to you, without any worries. Please accept my love, and show me how to serve you. Through my love for you, I am transformed and renewed.

There's something magical about your eyes. When I look into your eyes, I am filled with emotions. Your love touches me so deeply that it becomes difficult to hide my tears of joy. I get lost in the depth and the beauty of your eyes. Your eyes reflect a love so pure, it makes me feel secure. The way you look at me is like a warm hug. At that time, I feel loved so much and forget all my worries.

Loving you is not just a feeling, but a way of living. It guides my thoughts, words, and deeds, and it leads me towards doing what's right. Every moment spent in your presence is a gift, and every memory of you is engraved in my heart forever. The thought of you brings me happiness and gives me the strength to face any challenge. With you as my guide, I feel unstoppable, and nothing seems too hard to overcome.

I can't believe how much you love me all the time. But sometimes, I worry that I can't love you back enough. I feel like I'm not good enough and that makes me nervous. I really want to love you as much as you love me, but I don't know how to. Please show me the way and help me get closer to you. Please help me to overcome my fears and insecurities so that I can love you with all my heart.

I don't want power, wealth, or fame, I just want to love you. I don't ask for anything from you except your grace, which is the greatest blessing. I pray that my love for you always grows and that it helps me let go of my worldly desires. Please help me be happy with whatever you give me, knowing that it's for my own good. May my love for you keep growing stronger, burning away my impurities and making me love you more.

Your love is like rain that falls on the earth, giving life to all that grows. It is like the gentle dew that settles upon the grass, reviving it and bringing it back to life. Without your love, I am like a dried plant, dying for lack of water. But with your love, I am like a thriving garden, filled with beauty and life. I am grateful for the rain of your love that falls upon me every day. Please keep raining your love on me forever.

If your love were a star, mine would be several constellations. If your love were a drop of water, mine would be an unending ocean. If your love were a mountain, mine would be many peaks. If your love were a flame, mine would be a strong passion. If your love were a single melody, mine would be a lovely harmony. If your love were a book, mine would be an entire library full of pages to read. If your love were a journey, mine would be a joyful adventure.

I wish I could give you the world, but all I have to offer is my love. I hope that my love for you is enough because it comes from the bottom of my heart. I give you my soul, knowing that it belongs to you. I don't have any gifts to offer, but I pray and show my devotion to you. You're the center of my universe, and my love for you is what drives me. I offer my love to you as your servant, and it's what gives me strength.

Loving you with the expectation of fulfilling my desires is not loving you at all. It's like I'm using you to get what I want, and that's not right. Instead, I want to love you purely and selflessly, without expecting anything in return. My love for you flows like a river, not to reach an end, but to sing its joy all the way. I want to focus on learning to love you for who you are, rather than for what you can do for me.

You are the start and end of everything in my life. My love for you will never go away, rather it grows stronger with every passing day. You light up my life like the sun and moon and guide me every time, everywhere. You are the answer to all my prayers. I think of you every single day. No matter how many ups and downs I face, my love for you will keep growing.

Though I can't see your love with my eyes, I feel it all around me, every moment of my life. I feel it in the beating of my heart, the smile of a stranger, the sweet scent of flowers, and the cheerful chirping of birds. I feel it in the beauty of your creation, the greatness of your power, and the wonder of your mercy. And even in times of pain, struggle, or success, I know your love is there, guiding and lifting me. Thank you for your endless love, for it's the light that brightens my days and fills my heart with joy.

I see you in everything and everyone around me. I see you in the busy city among the crowds, and in the beautiful starry night sky that fills me with wonder. I hear your divine song in the rhythm of raindrops, the laughter of children, the rustling of the leaves, and the gentle flowing of the stream. Every sight, sound, and sensation in the world reminds me of your infinite presence.

Your love has transformed me as a caterpillar transforms into a beautiful butterfly. Just as a butterfly spreads its wings and takes flight, your love empowers me to live a life of purpose and reach for my dreams. I am truly blessed by your love and the gift of transformation that comes with it. Thank you for always being with me, and guiding me through every change and transformation.

Everything around us—sun, moon, stars, mountains, and oceans—is a sign of your power and love. It is a constant reminder of your infinite love and compassion for everyone. Everything in this world is a part of your divine plan. With your love and guidance, I have learned to overcome negative feelings and thoughts. My heart is filled with love from you, and I don't have any room for hate or negativity. I see everything as sacred and special, and I respect and appreciate every part of your creation.

Your love is so big that it can't be measured or contained. It is beyond my understanding but I feel blessed to have it. Your love has the power to transform everything. It is available to anyone who seeks it. Your love is a powerful force that purifies and cleanses everything it touches. It burns away all the bad stuff, leaving only what is pure and good. Your love brings light into darkness, hope into despair, and life into death.

My heart is like a garden waiting for your touch. I am a humble gardener seeking your love and care to help me prosper. Please nourish the soil of my soul with your wisdom and understanding, and help me grow in faith and devotion. With your loving care and guidance, I am filled with hope that my heart's garden will flourish into a beautiful place where your divine presence is felt by all who enter, filling their hearts with peace, love, and joy.

Your love is like a never-ending river that flows towards me constantly. Whenever I feel empty, I reach out to your love to fill me up again. Your love never runs dry, no matter how much I draw from it. Your love always refreshes me, giving me new life and energy. I flow on your endless river, eyes wide with wonder. Every turn brings a happy sight, each splash a special sound. I laugh, I dream, I whisper to the stars, carried by your gentle hand. You're the wind in my hair, the sun on my cheek, the light in the dark.

Your love is more than just a feeling. It is a never-ending flow of care and tenderness that sustains me through every moment of my life. Your warmth surrounds me, envelopes me, and fills me with an indescribable sense of peace and joy. With your love, I never feel alone, lost, or afraid. In your hug, I grow like a flower reaching for the sun, my problems disappear like snowflakes on a warm hand. No darkness can reach me, no strong wind can shake my roots, because your love holds me steady like the bottom of the ocean.

In your divine presence, I have learned the true meaning of love and the beauty of selflessness. I have realized that love is not a transaction, but rather a sacred bond that exists between us all. It is not about what I can gain from others, but rather what I can give to others. It's a powerful force that can heal and guide me through tough times. Please continue teaching the value of true love to help me always put others before myself.

How blessed I am to have your love! Your love is the wind that carries me through new experiences, the gentle push that encourages me to try new things, and the warm embrace that makes me feel safe. You are my safe place, where I can find comfort and security, knowing that you are always there to help me when I stumble and fall. Your love has shown me that anything is possible and that with you by my side, I can face any challenge.

No one in this world has my heart like you do, and there is no one I love more than you. No one can even match the depth of my devotion to you. You are the highest power for me, and the roots of my love for you run deep, unbreakable, and strong. No one can ever replace you in my heart, and my devotion to you is the purest and most sincere. I pray that you always accept my humble love and devotion to you.

I really, really love you a lot, and I want your help to love you even more. Please make sure my love for you stays strong and never stops, and help me love you more each day. When I'm with you, I feel calm and happy, so please help me keep on loving you all the time. Your love is super important to me, and the best way to feel even happier is to keep loving you more and more every single day.

I pray that my love for you grows even bigger, like a tree that reaches the sky, getting stronger as the days go by.

You're the reason I wake up happy, with a heart full of thanks. I've given myself to you entirely, and every day, I aim to love you more, in every possible way.

I don't want anything back for loving you so much; just being with you is more than enough. Your love in my life is an honor, and I'm grateful every day to have you by my side.

I'm not scared of losing things because my love for you is the most important, like a treasure that will never fade or diminish.

As a flower turns towards the sun, getting energy from its warmth and light, I turn to you, looking for goodness for my soul. I can't take my thoughts away from you for even a second, because you are where all the good and pure things come from. I give my life to you like a flower opens its petals to the world. In this dance with my open petals, I want to give my life as a gift to everyone, and it's all because of your kindness.

Your affection for me is immeasurable, immense, and boundless, like the universe itself. It's an endless sea of feelings that cannot be contained or calculated by anything in this world. Just as the universe is composed of countless atoms, your love is made up of countless lovely and exceptional qualities that make me feel cherished and valued. In each atom of your love, there's something special I discover—a hidden gem. It's like finding a small piece of kindness, a gentle touch of grace, and a bit of happiness that ties everything together.

Your love is big and wide like an ocean that goes on forever. It's hard for me to understand, but I know you love me so much. I feel really small, like a tiny boat in a huge ocean. But I know you see me, and that makes me feel safe. You're the captain, guiding me through everything. Your love is like the waves that wash over me and make me feel new again. Thank you for your love that never changes.

I thank you for the love that beats in my heart for you. Your love is like a melody that echoes within me, bringing peace and serenity to my soul. I pray that this melody continues to play within me, always reminding me of your constant love. Let the melody of your love be the rhythm that gives me strength and hope every time. Help me to always hear this beautiful melody, and make it a part of who I am.

When I look at the flowers, trees, and animals around me, I see your love and creativity in everything you've made. And then, I think about myself—with a heart that loves, a mind that thinks, and a soul that cherishes you. Thank you for creating me in your image and giving me special qualities that make me who I am. I want to use these qualities to serve you and make you proud. Please guide me so that I can bring glory to your name in everything I do.

My love for you is like a big, exciting wave of feelings that I can't hold back, and I wouldn't even want to try. It's like my heart has its little mind, and it always wants to be close to you, just like a magnet sticks to metal.

It's this strong pull that makes me feel so connected to you like my heart knows you're the special one it wants to be with all the time.

This love doesn't need a special reason; it's just there, and I'm thankful for it every day. It's a feeling that's hard to put into words, but it's a feeling I never want to go away.

Your love is like the roots of a tree, going down deep into my heart. Just as the roots of a tree help the tree to grow and blossom, your love helps me to become a better person each day. Your love is like the food that the roots take from the earth, giving me the strength and energy to face any challenges. Your love is like the sunshine and rain that contribute to my personal growth. Thank you for being my constant support, like the roots that keep the tree standing tall and firm.

Just like a tree offers shade to tired travelers, your love protects me from overwhelming sadness, giving me comfort and new energy. It nurtures feelings of care, kindness, and understanding in me, allowing them to grow and bring goodness into my relationships with others. Just as the leaves of a tree absorb sunlight, your love absorbs my worries and fears, transforming them into hope and optimism. It breathes life into my spirit, infusing me with a renewed sense of purpose and strength.

You are like a rainbow that appears after the rain. It's like a magical painting in the sky, full of bright colors that make everything feel happy and hopeful. As the colors of the rainbow come together to form a beautiful sight, your warmth weaves together all the different aspects of my life to create a beautiful fabric filled with love. Your love is like all the colors in a rainbow, and each color is like a special piece of how awesome and wonderful you are.

I deeply desire you every day, like a thirsty man in a desert searching for water. I keep thinking about being with you, like a person in a big desert hoping to find a cool, refreshing place. Your being there is like that soothing, cool water that brings relief to my heart. Without you, it's as if I'm wandering through the dry, sandy lands, wishing for the comfort only your presence can bring. My hunger for you intensifies with each passing moment, as I recall the depth of your empathy and kindness.

Every decision I make, every step I take, is influenced by the love I have for you. My heart beats with the rhythm of our love, and every breath I take is filled with the sweet fragrance of our memories. I carry this love with me, like a precious gem, always valued and kept close to my heart. The very thought of you fills me with warmth, like the radiance of your holy presence. You are the missing piece of my soul, the one that completes my life.

Just like the universe, my love for you expands and evolves endlessly. Every day, it grows and changes, evolving into something even greater. Imagine the universe with all its stars and galaxies; well, my love for you is even deeper and wider than that. The universe, as huge as it is, seems small compared to how much I love you. It's like my feelings for you go way beyond what we can see in the vast space of the sky. My love for you is timeless and eternal. It will continue to burn bright and strong, even as the stars in the sky begin to fade.

Just the thought of you keeps me up, a rush of energy flowing through me, making it hard to sleep. Whenever I close my eyes, I enter a world where all I see is you. Each breath I take is filled with the essence of your love as if the air itself reminds us of our deep connection. In this mystical space, time seems to pause, and every whispered prayer, every tender touch of devotion, becomes a cherished melody, playing softly in the depths of my soul.

Your love is like a calm and gentle waterfall that flows down rocks covered in moss. It helps to remove the marks of bitterness and anger from my heart. The comforting sounds of the waterfall make the painful memories fade away. It cleans my heart, making me feel clear and refreshed. Just like how a waterfall's continuous movement shapes the land it passes through, your love shapes and changes me. It creates new paths for me to grow and discover myself. It inspires me to embrace change and accept the person I am becoming.

When I look into your eyes, I'm gently reminded of the way love brings sweetness to our lives, just like honey gently pouring over a flower. Being with you is like being wrapped in a comforting blanket of affection and tenderness. Your love acts as a magnetic force, pulling me closer to you, much like a bee drawn to the beauty of the blooming flower. Our bond is amazing like a bee moving gracefully from one flower to another. It's like a dance of closeness, where each time we interact is as sweet as a bee discovering nectar in a new flower.

Just like a tree without flowers isn't pretty to look at, my heart would be lonely without the brightness of your love. Without your love, I'd be like a tree without any fruits of kindness, compassion, and understanding. Your love is like a soft wind that talks gently through the leaves, sharing messages of admiration and loyalty. It's as if the whispers of the wind carry sweet words of affection, creating a calming melody in the branches of our connection. Each rustle of the leaves becomes a love note, expressing the deep bond we share.

You are so beautiful. Your beauty is like the rain that falls softly during the rainy season. Just as raindrops come from the sky, your radiance fills my heart with joy. Even when it's hot in the summer, the hope of rain brings relief. Similarly, thinking about you makes me feel better. When rain falls, it brings life to the land, making flowers grow and turning dry fields into green, fertile places. In the same way, your kindness and love bring new life to my spirit.

Before I found you, I used to wonder if real, pure love was possible. I wanted a love that went beyond just human desires and selfish connections, a love that was selfless and divine. And then I found you. Being with you showed me how love can be there in everything you do, every kind word you say, and every moment we share with devotion. It's the way you listen with understanding, the warmth in your smile, and the genuine care in your actions that make love tangible and real.

When I see you, I smile without even knowing why. It happens naturally, without any specific reason. Our presence is like sunshine breaking through the clouds, bringing warmth to my heart. It's a spontaneous reaction, a burst of joy that lights up my day. You have a special power to make me feel incredibly happy. My heart fills with joy and I can't help but smile brightly. You are the reason for this happiness. You paint my life like beautiful artwork, using laughter and pure delight as your brushes. My soul is grateful for you.

You spread love to so many people. How do you shower the same love? Only you can perform such amazing things. You ignore people's faults and are always there to help them. You have such a caring nature. Even if people remember you only when they need something, you ignore their selfishness as their childish behavior. Only you possess such wisdom. You're good at understanding how people feel and being there for them when they need someone to talk to.

All I want from you is more and more love, without asking for anything else. It makes me so happy like nothing else can. I want to gather every moment of your love, like collecting the most beautiful gems, and keep them safe in the collection of our shared memories. So just give me your love, and I will cherish it forever. With your love, I am complete. Let your love flow through me. All I ask is to be consumed by your love, to be enveloped in its divine embrace. In your love, I find infinite bliss and am eternally blessed.

Just like how clear water satisfies our physical thirst and cleanses our bodies, I want the pureness of your love to clean my inner self. Your love, like crystal-clear water, has the power to wash away the worries and doubts that stick within me. Let it flow through the channels of my heart, sweeping away any negativity and leaving behind a refreshed and calm spirit. With each drop of your pure love, create waves of peace that touch every corner of my being, bringing a deep sense of happiness and satisfaction.

Your eyes are like an ocean, beautiful and mystical. Whenever I look into them, I get lost in their depth and discover something new and fascinating every time. The more I look into your eyes, the more connected I feel with you. In your eyes, I see a reflection of myself. It's a place where I find my safe space. A place where I'm accepted with an open heart. All I want is to see the world through your eyes.

My love for you goes beyond what makes sense, like a lively song playing on a magical stage. It is a pure and flawless feeling that cannot be fully absorbed by human understanding. When I am in your presence, everything fades away, and my heart overflows with joy and thankfulness. It's as if you have created me to be fully yours, and I feel complete and content in your divine embrace. The love I have for you is the most sincere and genuine expression of my faith.

Your love is as pure as clear dewdrops on flower petals. In these tiny balls of purity, I can see how much you love me. It's a love that is very pure and peaceful. It's like when little drops of water gather on leaves in the morning, making everything sparkle and adding a touch of magic to the day, just like your love does for me. Each time you show me your affection, my heart opens up and becomes more vibrant, just like a flower opening up and showing its beautiful emotions.

Surrender

Whatever I have got, I have got it from you only. Whatever I have to give, I have to give it to you only. What I get is not mine, and what I give is also not mine. Whatever is there is all yours. Whatever I get or give, that also is yours. I am yours. Whatever I am doing, I am doing all that for you only. I just bow down at your lotus feet and seek your grace for the rest of my life.

I am so lost in you that I don't even consider the thought of losing myself in you. Now, day and night, only you appear before me. I can't imagine ever losing you. I feel overwhelmed by my emotions for you, and I can't escape your captivating presence. Interacting with others may feel like a routine, but our relationship is something truly unique. In misunderstandings, people consider themselves superior to you. But when someone becomes yours, they understand everything.

I'm grateful to be in your hands, like a piece of clay in the hands of a skilled potter. You know how to shape me into something beautiful and useful. I trust your wisdom to mold me into the best version of myself. Just like the potter uses the wheel to shape the clay, I want to feel your gentle touch guiding me through life's twists and turns. Despite the pressure at times, I know you're refining me, and I appreciate your loving work in my life.

I come before you like a leaf falling from a tree. Just as a leaf trusts that it'll be caught and guided to where it needs to be, I trust that you'll lead me on my path with grace. As I fall from the branches high above, I release all my fears and doubts into your hands. Just like leaves play a role in nurturing the earth, I also believe that I have a purpose and contribution to make in this world. Please help me to discover my true calling and to use my unique gifts and talents to make a positive impact on the world.

Like a blank page waiting to be written, I stand before you with an open heart, eager to receive your direction. Please fill these empty spaces with your words of hope, comfort, and strength. In the future, I hope to see the beauty of your work on these pages and feel grateful for the journey that brought me here. Thank you for the gift of a blank page, and I promise to use it to glorify your name by filling it with actions that reflect your wisdom and love.

Like humming bees are attracted to a lotus flower, I feel attracted to your lotus feet. Your feet are like a magnet for my heart. They are the source of infinite joy and bliss, and I am eternally grateful for the opportunity to surrender myself at your feet.

I can't resist the attraction, and with every step towards your feet, I feel a deep connection, like the sweet nectar that captivates the bees.

I am your humble servant seeking protection in your feet from the troubles of the world. I want to serve you, hear your stories, and see your beautiful feet so that I can become pure and love you even more.

Life is like a dance, and it feels like you're the one showing me the steps. You know the moves and the music, and I'm happy to follow your lead. It's like you're the best dance partner, guiding me through the twists and turns of life's rhythm. Sometimes, I stumble and don't quite get the dance right. But you're always there to lift me and help me keep going. Thank you for being the perfect dance partner in this beautiful dance of life.

I offer my heart to you as a blank canvas. I trust that you will create a masterpiece of my life with the colors of your divine love and wisdom. Each stroke of your brush will lead me to a greater purpose. I am ready to pour my heart into all the wonders and challenges that come with your artwork. Even when the colors seem dull and the brushstrokes hard, I know your infinite wisdom will lead me toward a brighter future.

Help me to remember that surrendering is not a sign of weakness, but a sign of my wisdom and strength. Give me the bravery to say, "I can't do it all," a bit like admitting that sometimes the river of life flows too fast for me to control.

Help me see that trying to control everything is like trying to catch the wind with my hands. Help me enjoy the adventure, where surprises make the story more fun.

Please show me that accepting and letting go of things I can't change can bring peace, clear thinking, and help me make better choices.

When I pray to you with a pure heart, I feel a sense of peace and clarity that is beyond all understanding. In your presence, I am reminded of my divine nature and the infinite potential that lies within me. You are the source of all love, compassion, and wisdom, and only by connecting with your divine presence I can experience the true depths of my own heart. You are the ultimate guide on my journey, and it is only through your grace that I can reach the heights of spiritual enlightenment.

Like a seed trusts the soil to grow, I trust your divine plan for me. It's like surrendering to the unseen, knowing that you have a beautiful plan in store. I am humbled to be a part of your plan. I am excited and hopeful for the journey ahead, believing that every step is guided by your wisdom and love. Just as a seed holds the potential for a vibrant flower, I feel the potential for growth and fulfillment in your divine plan. Thank you for choosing me to be a part of your divine plan.

I offer myself to you as a humble servant, ready to do what you want me to. Just like a flower needs time to grow and open up, help me stay calm and have faith in your timing. Like a flower unfolds its petals when the time is right, guide me to be patient and trust that things will happen when they're supposed to. Just as a flower's beauty takes time to fully show, help me understand that my life's journey will unfold gradually, with each moment playing a role.

Give me the strength to surrender myself to the present moment and your divine will. Help me become like a leaf, dancing on the river of today with joy and lightness. Teach me to be as flexible as the wind, bending gracefully with the twists and turns of fate. Help me release the heavy stones of past regrets and the worries of future storms. As I navigate the river of now, help me find strength in the face of the unknown, trusting that your plan leads me to new and meaningful destinations.

The fear of the unknown overwhelms me, and I don't know what lies beyond. It's like standing on the edge of something new, where what's ahead is hidden. But I trust that you are with me, guiding me through this uncertain journey. I place my faith in you, knowing that you will lead me towards a new beginning and the light. With your grace, I can face death without fear, as you are my ultimate protector and guide. Thank you for your love and mercy, and please always be with me.

I have come to realize that the answers to my questions and the solutions to my problems are revealed to me as I surrender to your divine grace. Please help me to let go of my doubts, fears, and worries, and to trust in your infinite wisdom and love. Guide me to be patient and devoted in my faith, knowing that you will always provide for me and lead me in the right direction. Thank you for your never-ending love and compassion.

Just like a bicycle rider moves through twists and turns, I trust you to guide me through life's ups and downs. I always look to you for help in staying balanced. I have faith in you and believe you will lead me where I need to go. Just like a bicycle chain keeps the wheels turning, I need to keep moving forward in my spiritual journey to stay connected to you. Life can be tough, but with you beside me, I can overcome anything.

Life gets noisy, and my mind feels like a busy marketplace, filled with worries and endless thoughts. So I give all these thoughts to you, knowing that you understand me better than I understand myself. Take away my worries and fears, and give me the strength to let go of my thoughts and feelings. Help me to find peace within myself and let my heart be open to your presence. Give me the courage to face my fears and overcome obstacles. Let me feel your grace and love, and be content with what I have.

My life is like a canvas and you are the artist painting your masterpiece. Your hand guides each stroke of the brush, and I trust that you are leading me towards my best life. Even when I don't understand the colors you choose, I know that you have a plan for my life that is greater than what I can imagine. Please help me to let go of my need for control and trust your divine artistry. Thank you for creating a beautiful masterpiece in my life and in the world around me.

My plans are small compared to your plans for my life. It's easy for me to get caught up in my timetable, thinking that my timing is the best. Please help me to remember that your plans are better for me. I believe that your timing is perfect, even if it doesn't match my ideas of timing. Please bring people into my life who will support and encourage me as I try to do what you want me to do.

My thoughts and actions have brought me a lot of pain. I realized that trying to control everything didn't make my life better; instead, it made things more complicated. I admit that this desire for control often led to problems and made me feel lost. Help me to let go of my desires and attachments, and to find happiness in serving others and following your path. Please give me the wisdom to see beyond this world's illusions, the strength to overcome my limitations, and the grace to act wisely.

I offer my entire being to your feet, knowing that my devotion to them is the highest form of worship. Your feet are like the gateway to a world that is filled with infinite love, grace, and beauty. I will always cherish and honor your feet as they lead me towards eternal happiness. May your divine feet always remain the center of my existence, and may I continue to offer my love and devotion to them forever.

I trust you completely like a sailor trusts the sea. You guide me like stars guide a sailor through the dark. Just as a sailor finds comfort in the calmness of the sea after a long journey, I know that with you by my side, I can find a sense of peace and relief in even the most troubling times. Like a sailor's journey, my journey will have its challenges, but I trust that you will help me overcome them.

Please help me understand that worldly events are extremely insignificant and allow me to be unattached to them. Guide me to see the broader view and the important parts of life. Whether I'm happy or sad, I just want to focus on the good feeling of being devoted to you. Keep my mind always thinking about you and not going off in other directions. Even if it does, I hope it only feels your presence, which is my beloved heart, and nothing else.

I need your help to stop seeking approval and validation from others, so I can fully accept and feel your love, no matter what. Give me the courage to trust in my worthiness and honor my true self, even if others don't understand or appreciate me. Help me see myself the way you do, recognizing the unique person you created me to be. Open my eyes to the special gifts and talents you've showered upon me. Give me the power to use my gifts for good and make a real difference.

I don't have all the answers, and what I know about the world is just from what I've seen and think. There's so much more out there that I haven't learned or experienced yet. Help me be open to new things and different ideas. I want to grow and understand more, with your help. Show me the way to true wisdom and peace inside. As I go, keep me humble and willing to listen. Help me let go of what I think I know and be ready for new perspectives.

I hand over my past mistakes and things I feel sorry about to you. I'm sure that, with your love and help, I can let go of these heavy feelings and go ahead on the road to getting better and growing. I believe you'll guide me right and show me how to become a better person. Give me the strength to deal with any tough times and to learn from what went wrong. Help me stay focused on now and the future, finding meaning and purpose in my life.

With your divine hand in mine, I discovered a strength I never knew existed, pushing me beyond my old boundaries. Your sacred touch, like a balm, healed the wounds of my past. Everything I am, and everything I will become, finds its purpose and wholeness within the grip of your hand, leading me on an extraordinary journey of self-discovery and boundless love. With time, and with the support of a faithful partner like you, I am sure to emerge from the darkness, stronger and better than ever before.

My deep feelings for you go beyond any limits or boundaries, existing in a place that is hard to understand. Your presence touches every part of me, and my commitment to you is more than just a role or title. It's like a strong connection that runs through my heart, affecting how I think and act. You have a big influence on my life, shaping how I see the world and how I go through it. No label or job description can show how much you mean to me.

I don't know where I came from or where I'll go. But what I do know is that I can feel you near, and I'm aware of your presence. It's like a comforting hug, making me feel that I'm not alone. Even though I'm unsure and confused, my devotion to you remains strong. Though the journey ahead may be unknown, I draw strength from the certainty that you are with me. Deep inside, I have a strong desire to be connected with your everlasting brightness.

Every bit of your name has a powerful and meaningful vibe that connects with me. Your name becomes a magical mantra, filling me with endless energy and optimism. It's like a special spell that lifts my mood and makes me feel more positive about life.

When I say your name, it's as if a burst of good vibes runs through me, giving me a fresh sense of hope and an infectious excitement that helps me face challenges.

Your name isn't just a bunch of sounds; it's like a boost of strength that keeps me going with a strong sense of positivity.

You have all the power to control what happens. Nothing can happen without your approval. I trust in your plan and give up control to follow your wishes. It makes me feel peaceful knowing that you are in charge and that everything happens according to your perfect plan. At every moment, I depend on your permission to show me the way. Whenever I make a choice, I understand that it's ultimately your decision. I know you see things better than I do, and you always want what's best for me.

In your surrender, I find freedom. It's like a heavy burden is taken away, and I can be completely genuine without any limitations. You are the ultimate source of strength, love, and guidance. In your surrender, I find comfort and peace, knowing that you are there to take care of me. It helps me let go of society's expectations and be my real self. I don't have to pretend or hide anymore. I can just be true.

Nothing belongs to me. Everything in this world, everything I have, actually belongs to you. It's like I'm just borrowing these things for a while. You are the one who truly owns everything, and I am just a humble caretaker of the good things you give me. I am just a small piece in the bigger picture of the universe. I no longer feel like I own things, but instead, I feel thankful for the blessings and talents you have given me.

Every time your name is heard, it feels like my heart is saying it over and over again. Your love runs through my veins, giving life to the deepest parts of my heart. My heart moves to the rhythm of your love, syncing with every beat of yours. It has become a container, overflowing with emotions that are only meant for you. My heart no longer belongs to me alone; it belongs to you, forever connected in the fabric of our love.

I offer myself completely to you like a dry leaf surrendering to the direction of the wind. Whether the wind lifts me to unknown heights, pushes me forward on a purposeful path, or brings me back through challenges, my faith remains strong. Even if the wind drops me to the ground, I don't lose hope, because I believe your grace is there to lift me again. I trust your plan, knowing that every fall is a chance to grow, change, and become closer to you.

You have taken away my worries and made them your own. You rescued me and kept me safe. Why should I go to someone else when you have made me your own? Now, whenever I feel anxious, I come to you, and I find peace at your doorstep. I completely involve myself in your special and amazing activities, experiencing them as if I'm right there. I have always called upon your name because you have accepted me as your own.

I feel a strong desire to dedicate myself completely to serving you. It doesn't matter where I am or what's going on around me because my ultimate joy comes from committing myself to you completely. My journey is not limited by physical boundaries but by how much I care for your well-being. By serving you, I discover a strong sense of purpose that goes beyond everyday life, and it brings me deep contentment.

My biggest wish is to be close to you, and I truly believe that saying your name can make it happen. When I hear your name, I want to vanish, happily becoming part of the surrender dance. Chanting your name is like opening a door to a place where dreams and reality meet. The more I repeat it, the more I see that the usual limits of what can happen stretch into something much bigger. Your name seems like a magical key that unlocks endless possibilities, and in surrendering to it, I find a world of wonders.

I don't want to be famous or known for following you. I just want to be humble as I live my life. I want to be simple and show a lot of respect, knowing that real dedication comes from being genuinely humble. By being a dedicated follower of yours, I want to feel close to your special essence and let your wisdom guide me. I hope it lights up my way, bringing me peace inside and making me feel spiritually complete.

As I surrender, my devotion grows stronger. It's a way of recognizing that you are in charge of my life and its direction. Through surrender, I open myself to receive your divine grace. I let go of my expectations, recognizing that I'm not in control, and trust in the greater plan of the universe. Through surrender, I become humble and accept both successes and failures, knowing that they are all part of your loving design.

I have a purpose in life, and that purpose is you. You're like the missing piece that completes the puzzle of my existence. Before our paths crossed, there was an unanswered question about the meaning of my journey. But with you, it's as if the universe whispered, "Here is where you belong." Your presence has given my life a profound sense of direction and meaning. Now my life's objective is to serve you, love you, cherish you, and grow and learn with you.

Whatever is happening in my life is happening for a reason. I don't know the reason and I don't want to know the reason. But I know it's happening by your grace. Whatever you are doing, you are doing it right. I do not understand the workings of the material world. So I depend on your divine power to help me sail through life's challenges.

I am your instrument. Hold me in your hand and play a tune that ignites my inner being with your devotion. I am eager to become engrossed in your music. Keep me close to your heart so that whenever I fail, you can guide me with your divine touch towards the right path. You are the master, and I'm ready to learn from you. I want to be your tool and create music that touches people's souls.

I don't need power or control, but I want to serve you with all my heart. I will try my best to be humble and simple because true greatness comes from selflessness, not from showing off. I find joy in quietly serving you, even if no one notices. I'm grateful for the opportunity to assist and serve someone as important as you. Being around you reminds me that it's better to be humble and focus on serving rather than seeking attention for myself.

The names and roles I've given myself are holding me back from knowing my true self. I've stuck myself in a small box, thinking these labels tell the whole story. But deep down, I understand they're just temporary and don't capture who I am. With your help and encouragement, I think I can break free from these labels and understand you more deeply. I'm asking for your guidance to let go of these labels and help me see my real self.

Gratitude

I'm grateful to you for everything in my life, whether it was good or hard. Instead of saying 'bad', I prefer to use 'hard' because I've come to understand that even the difficult times were important for my growth. Each experience, whether positive or challenging, has been a building block in shaping who I am. Difficult situations taught me to be tough, happy moments taught me to be grateful, and the people I met showed me how to be compassionate and kind.

I don't feel like asking you for anything anymore, what should I ask for? You have already given me a lot. I feel embarrassed to ask for more from myself when I think about all the things I have already taken from you. You've been kind, giving me so many good things. Your generosity has made my days colorful. Now, I just stand quietly in front of you, thinking about how I can give back and share the good things you've given me.

You are more concerned about me than I am, as you have sent me into this world. You created who I am, made me alive, and helped me grow. Since the moment I was born, you've been looking after me with great care. You have seen me succeed and fail, be happy and sad. Your constant care and concern have shaped me into the person I am today. The bond we have is extraordinary, based on love, trust, and understanding.

You woke me up today because you think there are still things I need to do and learn in this world. I have another day to learn more and have new experiences while following your guidance. You woke me up today because you believe in what I can do, even when I don't believe in myself. You encourage me to do more than I think I can, to do things that are beyond ordinary, and to embrace extraordinary things.

You are the one who does everything, you are the one who makes others do everything. It's even difficult for me to take a single breath without you. You are the one who puts me to sleep, you are the one who wakes me up. You are the reason I grow and change. In this journey of life, you are my perfect companion. You are the most important part of who I am, my inspiration, my everything.

Even when my tears flow like a river, and my fears make me feel trapped, I find comfort in knowing that I'm not alone. You give me a safe place where I can shed my tears and face my fears without feeling judged or ashamed. You help me realize that it's okay to feel scared or overwhelmed at times. I appreciate your reminder that my tears can help release pain and my fears can be a catalyst for growth.

Thank you for the time you have given me on this earth. I want to make the most of it by living a life that aligns with your purpose for me. It is easy to get caught up in the opinions and expectations of others, but I know that this is not the path to true happiness and fulfillment. With your help, I am committed to staying true to myself and using the unique gifts and talents you have given me.

Every time the sun rises, my affection for you is renewed. And every time it sets, I am grateful for the day we have spent together. Even when the day is finished, my heart continues to beat with the rhythm of our love. And I know that tomorrow when the sun rises again, I will love you even more than I do today. Because with every sunrise and every sunset, my love for you is reborn, and my thankfulness for the time we share grows stronger with each passing moment.

Your grace and love can't be touched or seen, but I can feel it deep inside me. Your presence is not something I can touch, but I can feel it with every beat of my heart. Your wisdom is not something I can hold, but I can sense it within me. The wonders of your creation are not just things I can see but also feel in my heart. Your divine presence feels like a warm hug that I can feel in my heart, even when I'm alone. Your blessings are not things I can hold, but they bring me peace and joy in my heart.

Like a loyal bee, I'm buzzing with joy as I happily fly through the beautiful garden of your divine love. With my wings gently moving, I eagerly collect the sweetness of devotion, going from one flower to another, in search of the very essence of your divine grace.

Your presence attracts me like a bee to the most aromatic flower, constantly mesmerized by the irresistible scent of your limitless love. Just like the bee collects pollen, I gather moments of prayer and worship, filling the depths of my heart with the abundance of your blessings.

You're like the sunshine that makes my days bright, the breeze that lifts my spirits, and the rain that feeds my inner self. When I'm feeling stressed, just having you around calms me like a comforting balm. Your love is like a strong anchor that keeps me stable during life's challenges, a guiding light that shows me the way, and a protective shelter that keeps me safe. I'm thankful for the strength, motivation, and peace you give me.

When I think about my life, I realize that big achievements and things I own don't make me happy. It's the small things that happen every day that bring me joy. I ask for your help in valuing these small moments and making them important in my heart. These moments add up and make my life rich in ways that money can't. Please keep reminding me of their value so that I never forget how important they are to me.

You light up my life like the stars in the night sky, giving me comfort and warmth. Every moment with you feels like a dream come true, brightening up everything around me. You are my safe place, my home, my everything. Being with you makes me feel like the luckiest person in the world. Without you, my life would be dark and empty like a starless sky, but with you, it's like a lovely night that I never want to end.

You bring a melody to my life that's sweeter than anything I've ever heard. Your melody is not just a sound but a feeling, connecting with the deepest chords of happiness within me. Your presence is like a beautiful song that plays in my heart, creating a soundtrack of joy and warmth. I find myself humming along to the tune of our shared experiences, and each note is a special reminder of the joy you, the divine, have brought into my life.

You bring so much color and life to my world like a flower blooming in the morning sun. You are the reason why my heart beats, and without you, I would feel lost in this world. Every moment with you is like a canvas being painted with the most vibrant and beautiful colors. You have a way of brightening up even the darkest corners of my world. Just the thought of you makes me expand swell with love and joy.

Just like how the sun rises every day, bringing light and warmth to the world, your divine presence in my life lights up my heart and soul, filling me with your love and kindness. It reminds me that there is a higher power looking out for me, keeping me safe, and giving me the strength to handle life's challenges. I'm always thankful for your presence because it has changed my life in ways I never thought possible.

You have a purpose for me, a purpose that I seek to discover and fulfill through your grace. Please help me to let go of my ego and surrender to your divine will, just as the ocean surrenders to the rhythm of the tides. I know that life can be unpredictable and challenging, but with your guidance, I will stay strong. Help me to embrace the ups and downs of life with an open heart and a humble spirit.

I feel very small when I think how huge the world is. Despite my smallness, you have given me the gift of life and the opportunity to serve you. It makes me happy to know that one day I'll merge with you and that I'll find my true purpose and be at peace in your loving arms. The thought of merging with you brings a sense of fulfillment and purpose, like a tiny drop joining a vast ocean. I'm not eagerly waiting for that day because I trust it will surely come.

I am like a tree planted in a desert, seeking the life-giving water that sustains it. I am lost without your divine grace and blessings. Just as a tree needs water to survive in the desert, I need your love and guidance to thrive in this world. May your love be the life-giving water that sustains me and helps me grow stronger in my faith. I surrender myself to your will and trust in your divine plan for my life.

In this world full of changes and chaos, I feel peaceful and safe in your presence. Your love for me never changes, and it is the only thing that remains constant. Even though life can be unpredictable, my belief in you never shakes because you are my anchor. Your love is the one thing that brings me hope and happiness, especially when everything around me seems to be changing. I am grateful for your love, which helps me stay strong in all circumstances.

Please help me to appreciate and be grateful for my life, no matter what's happening. When I'm thankful, you give me even more to be thankful for. Every time I think about you, I remember how blessed I am. I promise to focus on the good things in my life and trust that you'll make them even better. I want to celebrate everything, even the small things, because they are all important. Please help me to always remember to say thank you to you for everything you've given me.

Every moment is an opportunity to start fresh in your love. It's a chance for me to get closer to you, and I offer my heart and soul to you every moment. Each moment is a gift that allows me to let go of the past and begin again with your help. I am grateful for your love that surrounds me always. With each breath, I thank you for bringing me closer to you. I offer you my devotion and gratitude in every moment.

Fill my heart with a never-ending desire to hear and retell the stories of your divine play. When I learn more about you, it fills me with so much happiness and love that tears start rolling down my cheeks. The tears that come are not just tears of emotion but also a way to let out the big love I feel. I want others to feel the same way, so they too can be filled with joy and forget all their worries. I also want to sing songs of your love and mercy and offer myself completely to you.

Whenever I am lost, you are the one who guides me back to the path that leads to my true calling. Your words inspire me to believe in myself and pursue my dreams with passion and dedication. You hold the key to my true purpose because you understand my deepest desires and motivations. Without you, I would be lost in a sea of uncertainty and doubt. But in your presence, I feel a sense of clarity and direction that I cannot find anywhere else.

In life, where things can be uncertain, I've learned that time goes by quickly, like sand slipping through my fingers. Everything has the potential to be lost, making me feel empty and searching for meaning. In the middle of all these changes, I find comfort in you. You are a dependable and powerful source of hope. Being with you is like having a guiding light that's special and can't be replaced. Please stay with me forever, making each moment brighter with your comforting presence.

I'm grateful for the moments of joy and happiness that brighten my life, whether it's a beautiful sunset, a kind gesture, or a moment of laughter. Even simple pleasures like enjoying my favorite meal, the sight of a clear night sky filled with stars, the feeling of soft sand between my toes at the beach, the taste of a perfectly ripe piece of fruit, the crackling sound of a fireplace, or relaxing in bed fills me with joy and gratitude. Keep shining your light on me and guide me on my journey of faith and discovery.

Laughing, crying, and sharing experiences with you are unforgettable moments that I will always cherish. Laughing with you feels like I'm creating a joyful tune. Sharing tears reflects the deep trust and connection I have with you. The memories I make with you are important to me, and I never want to stop making them with you. Your company brings me so much happiness. I'm excited about the memories I'll create with you in the future. I want to keep making memories with you for as long as I live.

I do not know much about the world or its mysteries, but I do know one thing for sure—I am blessed because I am loved by you. Your love humbles me and fills me with gratitude. It's a gift that I could never earn or deserve, but you give it to me freely and without hesitation. Your love is always there for me, no matter what happens. It's like a steady light that never diminishes or fades away.

Your beauty is beyond anything I can find or have on earth. Your beauty comes from inside you, showing how much you love and care for everyone. When I'm close to you, all my desires for worldly things disappear, and I feel extremely satisfied and peaceful. I wish my eyes may be filled with the sight of your incredible beauty, and that my heart may always be devoted to you. Please bless me with the opportunity to see your beauty and feel the joy that comes with it.

Your mercy is like a gift from you that helps me know you better. It's like a special key that lets me feel close to you. Without it, there's no other way for me to understand your amazing nature. Every day, I remember how much you love me and never give up on me. Your kindness brings me comfort and gives me a fresh start. When I'm feeling very sad, your mercy lifts me and gives me hope, even in the darkest times.

You are a perfect mix of being strong and kind, serious and gentle. Your strength supports me when things get tough, and your kindness feels like a cool breeze on a warm day. I am lucky to witness these different sides of your divine nature.

Your power is so immense that it can shake the very foundations of the world, making everyone humble and aware of your control. Your seriousness reflects your commitment to fairness and doing what is right. Please help me always remember and appreciate the importance of your dual nature.

With you, I feel a sense of completeness and wholeness that I cannot find anywhere else in this material world. Your presence is like the warmth of the sun that melts away the coldness in my heart and fills it with your love and compassion. Your love is not limited by time or space. It flows freely and abundantly, enveloping me in a sense of peace and contentment. I always want to walk in the light of your divine presence.

In everything you do, there's something wonderful and special, and every choice you make adds to a beautiful and exceptional story. I'm grateful to be here, seeing all the amazing things that happen because of your endless kindness. It's like being part of a truly extraordinary tale, and I feel lucky to witness it all unfold. With a heart full of gratitude and deep respect, I offer myself to you, recognizing that you are the one who plans and controls everything in the world.

I'm truly grateful for your beautiful presence, like the refreshing rain. Just as rain brings a delightful scent to the air, your presence fills my life with a pure and divine fragrance. Each raindrop touching the ground reminds me of your gentle touch that washes away my sadness, leaving my soul refreshed and pure. Your beauty is like raindrops falling gently, waking up my senses and making everything around me seem brighter. I'm grateful for the joy and positivity you bring into my life, just like how rain brings life to the earth.

You have given me the gift of free will, allowing me to cherish and nurture my desires. Every moment, my heart is filled with hopes, dreams, and strong desires. I am driven to find happiness, success, love, and satisfaction in this wonderful world that you have created so generously. Even though I can wish for different things in life, only you have the power to make those wishes come true. You're the one who turns my dreams into reality, making everything work out in a way that fits into your bigger plan.

I am grateful for the world you have created, which is full of beauty that reflects your divine grace. Please guide me to see the beauty in everything, even in the most ordinary things. Help me to look beyond the surface and discover the hidden beauty in all things. Grant me the wisdom to appreciate the differences that make everyone unique. Let me recognize that true beauty comes from within and that every person is unique and special in their way.

Since you entered my life, everything has improved. You were always around, but it took me a while to realize your importance. Now the colors seem brighter, the music sounds sweeter, and the world feels like a more welcoming place. With you, even the simple tasks of daily life become acts of devotion. It's as if every aspect of life has been infused with a touch of magic because of you. With you by my side, life becomes a dance of love, where every step is filled with grace and passion.

Whatever I lose is meant to be, and whatever I receive is due to your kindness. When tough times come, I won't complain about what I have lost because it was supposed to happen. Instead, I will accept the lessons in each difficult situation, knowing they make me a better person. When things go well, I won't show off what I have achieved because I didn't do it all by myself; it will be due to your kindness and blessings that I receive these good things.

I don't know what kind of feeling this is, but ever since I realized your presence, everything has started to feel good. The world around me has changed, and everything seems more colorful and hopeful. Every moment I spend with you becomes a precious memory in my heart, like a delicate brushstroke on a beautiful painting. Even simple things bring me so much joy that I can't explain. I'm excited to see what other wonderful things will happen as I go on this journey with you.

Your name has a special ability to make me feel better. It's like a magic cure that helps me feel less sad and more at ease. Just hearing your name gives me hope and makes me forget about my problems. It's like a comforting hug that heals my hurts and makes me feel calm inside. In a world where life can be difficult, your name stands out as a bright light that shows me the way to happiness. It reminds me that even when things are tough, I have the guidance to overcome sadness and find happiness.

Your teachings have shown me how to let go and not get too attached to this temporary world. Every moment that goes by, things around me keep changing. It's like everything is always moving and nothing stays the same. I feel lucky to understand that the beauty of this world doesn't last forever. Through your kindness, I've learned that the real meaning of life is not about holding onto the things that don't last, but about embracing the everlasting truth within us.

You are the reason why I feel strong and confident. Without you, I am like a leaf that gets blown around by the wind. I realize my weaknesses and how small I am in the big picture of life. I don't have the strength to find my way on my own. I have no control over where I go or what I do. I feel like a ship without an anchor, drifting aimlessly. You have become my source of stability and guidance, inspiring me to achieve things I never thought possible.

When I'm around you, I feel at peace sharing this important truth. The essence of who I am, my very existence, is not a random accident but a precious gift given to me by you. Deep within me, there is a special spark, a small part of something sacred that makes up who I am. It's a gift that has a meaning, given to me with endless love and limitless wisdom. I accept the responsibility that comes with this precious gift. It's not enough to just receive it; I must honor it by how I think, speak, and act.

Some say you are not visible, but it's just you who shows up when no one else does. Seeing you isn't about using my eyes but about sensing you in my heart. It's in the quiet—my inner voice whispers to me, the gentle nudges of my conscience guiding me, and the strong experiences that are hard to explain. In the peaceful moments when I pray and my soul is calm, I can connect with the presence that lives inside me and all around me.

With your divine protection and support, sadness does not define who I am. Instead, it becomes a building block for my inner peace and growth. You are incredibly kind and understanding, giving me the space I need to experience my sadness and relying on your strength when mine weakens. In your loving embrace, sadness loses its power to overpower me. Instead, it serves as a reminder of how delicate and valuable life is. With your guiding hand above me, I find the bravery to face sorrow directly.

I know that I can't do anything for you, and you don't need anything from me. But you still created me. You gave me the gift of life and the chance to experience your grace and blessings. I didn't earn or deserve this gift, but you chose to give it to me anyway. I feel blessed to have the responsibility to honor and serve you. It's a privilege that I don't take lightly.

When I chant your name, I feel on top of the world. At that time, I forget everything else and get transported to a place where everything is possible. Your name has a rhythm that no one can match. With you, I'm filled with a sense of peace and contentment that I can't find anywhere else. Thank you for giving me the gift of your name. I'll always value it and hold it close to my heart.

You are the answer to all my questions. You are the solution to all my problems. You are the one who listens and understands me, you are the stability in my life. You come in my dreams as reality and you come in reality as dreams. Whichever path I walk, you are the destination. You add rhythm to my life. Without you, everything feels out of place, like a song with no beat. I can't imagine a life without you.

I am so grateful for the journey I have been on. Along the way, I have met amazing people who have made my life so much better. They have brought so much joy and goodness into my days. My family, friends, and mentors have been such a blessing. Please continue to bless these incredible people. Fill their lives with happiness, success, and fulfillment. Help them in their journeys and grant them strength and courage to pursue their dreams.

When I am with you, I prefer staying quiet. In the silence, I find a way of expressing feelings that don't need words—just the nice feeling of being with you and enjoying the calm. I cry a lot because I am so moved by how amazing you are. When you're around, I happily forget about everything else and focus only on you. I cover myself with the blanket of your emotions with closed eyes. I imagine a world where it's just you and me.

New Beginning

Even if you've gone through every part of this book until now, please realize that you're not at the end. In fact, you've only just begun to dig into the deep journey of prayers.

The point is, no matter how many times you read these prayers, there's always more waiting to be found. The words may stay the same, but it's your growth with each reading that breathes new life into them. As you go through the ups and downs of your life, facing new situations and welcoming fresh experiences, the prayers become a constant friend, growing with you.

Each time you come back to these pages is like opening a treasure chest with a new set of eyes. You bring a different point of view, shaped by your current feelings, thoughts, and questions. The prayers will give you new ideas, helping you feel more connected, and sharing the wisdom to handle the ever-changing challenges of your life.

It's like the prayers are in tune with the rhythm of your journey, adjusting to your changing needs. They act like a mirror, showing the progress within you, the strength gained through challenges, and the deeper understanding you've acquired. In this special relationship between reader and prayer, there's an ongoing exchange—a dance where the familiar words move with the growing soul.

So, every time you return to these pages, expect the unfolding of a unique chapter in your spiritual journey. Welcome the chance to discover sides of yourself you hadn't known before, and let the prayers be both a guide and a friend on this never-ending adventure of self-discovery. The words may look the same, but they carry the ever-changing waves of your life, giving comfort, guidance, and always refreshing your spirit.

Think of these prayers as tiny seeds you've planted in the garden of your heart—the special place inside you where all your feelings and thoughts grow. You've taken care of them by thinking good thoughts, feeling strong emotions, and being devoted.

Now, just like how a garden changes when it's spring, summer, fall, or winter, your connection with these prayers is going to change too. Every time you read them, it's like watching your garden bloom and grow. You'll discover new ideas, get help when things are tricky, and feel better when you're not sure about life situations.

So, just like you water plants to help them grow, keep reading these prayers, and watch your soul garden become more awesome with each reading. It's like having your own secret garden full of wisdom, and you're the amazing gardener!

Imagine this book as a massive, endless ocean, and each prayer inside is like a wave rushing to greet the shores of your thoughts and feelings. It's like standing on the beach, and as you read each prayer, it's as if you can feel the waves washing over you—strong, beautiful, and full of wisdom. It's like these waves are gently tickling the sandy shores of your mind and heart.

Now, here's the enchanting part: even though you've felt the impact of a wave (or a prayer) once, every time you read it again, it's like that wave is back, bringing with it its special energies and stories. It's like meeting an old friend who always has something new to share.

Just as the waves at the beach are never the same, each time you revisit a prayer, it's a different experience. The words remain constant, but your feelings, thoughts, and the situations in your life have changed. So, the wave of that prayer becomes unique each time, offering you fresh perspectives and insights.

It's like saying, "Hey, you've felt my presence before, but this time, I've got a new story to tell you, a new energy to share." So, reading these prayers is like a continuous dance with the waves, where each encounter is a unique and delightful experience.

Remember to keep your heart open and stay curious, which means being interested in all the cool stuff these prayers can teach you. Let the prayers be like a helpful guide as you explore your soul, which is like the deepest part of you.

You're in charge of your spiritual story. These prayers are like the tools you use to write your story. So, keep going, keep exploring, and have a blast on this awesome adventure with your prayers!

9 7 9 8 8 9 2 7 7 8 4 4 2